A TREASURY OF CLASSIC SEAFOOD RECIPES

by
Michelle A. Preston

JBG PUBLISHING
Los Angeles
Printed in the United States

TABLE OF CONTENTS

SHELLFISH

INTRODUCTION

Seafood and Your Nutrition

Consumers have known for years that fish and shellfish are among the healthiest types of food available today. Seafood provides a tremendous amount of protein for an extremely low number of calories. Three ounces of a lean fish, such as halibut, cod, or sole, contains less than 100 calories, yet offers approximately ⅓ to ½ of the U.S. recommended daily allowance of protein. The same is true for most shellfish.

The fat contained in fish and shellfish is, for the most part, polyunsaturated and monosaturated—much healthier, of course, than saturated fats. Additionally, many fish, particularly those heaviest in oil (trout, whitefish, salmon, tuna, etc.) contain a polyunsaturated fatty acid that helps lower cholesterol levels and prevent heart disease.

Low in sodium, fish and shellfish are also a valuable source for such vitamins and minerals as Vitamin B, iron, zinc, potassium, and others. Seafood is good for you and tastes good . . . it's the perfect nutritional source!

Choosing Fresh Fish

Buying fresh fish is actually a simple and easy task. For whole fish, make sure that the skin gives off a bright, clean sheen, while the scales remain tightly affixed to the skin. When pressed with a finger, the skin of a fish should bounce back immediately, leaving no indentation.

Additionally, the eyes of any fish should be clear and never cloudy. Finally, one of the most basic ways to check for freshness is with your nose. Fish should smell like the ocean: fresh and breezy. Any fish with a "fishy" or unpleasant smell, such as ammonia, should be rejected immediately.

When buying fillets, also look for a bright, clean sheen. Fillets should also have a fresh ocean smell and should never appear yellowish, gray, or dried out.

Tightly closed shells are the best indication of freshness for any of the hard shellfish (clams, mussels, and oysters). If the shells are slightly opened, they should close quickly when tapped with your finger. Lobsters and crabs should be kicking their legs and appear to be lively rather than sluggish.

The old wives tale that clams, mussels, and oysters should only be eaten during months that contain the letter "r" has been proven false by medical and nutritional experts. However, when collecting your own shellfish, it is important to check with the proper authorities—usually your local health department—that the area where you are harvesting is safe, and that the "red tide" condition is not in effect. During "red tide," many shellfish contain a poison that is extremely harmful to humans. As long as you buy your seafood at a reputable market, and follow the guidelines suggested above, you should not run into any health problems.

FISH

BAKED AND ROASTED

Baked Bluefish

1½ pounds bluefish fillets
1½ teaspoons virgin olive oil
dash of salt
freshly ground black pepper
3 tablespoons lime juice
2 large red onions, halved from root to stem and sliced thinly
2 oranges, peeled, sliced, and quartered
2 large fennel bulbs, chopped
⅔ cup fresh fennel greens, chopped

1) Slice the bluefish into four pieces and place in an oiled baking dish.

2) Season with salt and pepper, and sprinkle with lime juice.

3) Mix together the onions, oranges, and fennel bulbs, and sprinkle over the bluefish.

4) Bake in a 400 degree oven for approximately 10 minutes per inch of thickness (including the vegetables) or until fish flakes easily when tested with a fork.

Serves 4

Idaho Catfish

4 skinned, pan-dressed catfish
2 slices raw bacon, diced
⅓ cup minced onion
¼ cup minced green pepper
dash of salt
¼ teaspoon pepper
1 egg, beaten
1 cup fresh bread crumbs
2 slices bacon, halved crosswise
5 oz. whole kernel corn, drained
5 oz. creamed corn

1) Cook bacon in a frying pan until lightly browned. Remove and save 2 tablespoons of bacon drippings.

2) Place drippings, onion, and green pepper in frying pan, cooking until the vegetables are tender. Stir in salt, pepper, egg, bread crumbs, bacon, whole kernel corn, cream-style corn.

3) Place catfish in a well-oiled baking pan and stuff loosely with mixture.

4) Place one piece of bacon on top of each of the fish.

5) Bake at 350 degrees for 25 minutes or until fish flakes easily when tested with a fork.

Serves 4

Curried Flounder

1½ pounds frozen flounder, partly thawed
½ clove garlic, minced
2 medium onions, chopped
1 tablespoon butter or margarine
2 medium-size apples, pared, quartered, cored, and sliced
4 ounces tomato paste
1 teaspoon salt
1 teaspoon curry powder
dash of pepper
½ cup water

1) Cut the flounder into 4 pieces and place in a shallow baking dish.

2) Saute garlic and onions in butter until soft. Stir in the apples, tomato paste, salt, curry powder, pepper and water. Heat to boiling, stirring often. Pour over flounder and cover.

3) Bake fish at 350 degrees for 25 to 30 minutes, or until the fish flakes easily when tested with a fork.

Serves 4

Flounder with Belgian Endive

1 tablespoon melted butter or margarine
12 heads Belgian endive
3 ounces water
12 sole fillets (3 ounces each)
Salt
freshly ground white pepper
½ cup shallots, finely chopped
⅓ teaspoon dry tarragon
1½ cups chicken broth
1½ cups dry white wine
¾ cup whipping cream

1) Place melted butter, endive and water in a frying pan over medium flame. Cover and cook, turning often, for until endive is tender, approximately 15 minutes. Let stand.

2) Season the flounder fillets with salt and pepper. Place an endive head on one end of each fillet and roll up. Set the rolls, seam sides down, in an oiled, shallow baking dish.

3) Cover and bake in a 400 degree oven for approximately 10 minutes or until fish flakes easily when tested with a fork.

4) In the pan used to cook the endive, combine shallots, tarragon, chicken broth and wine. Boil, uncovered, over high flame for 10 minutes. After flounder is cooked, drain the juices from the baking dish into the wine mixture. Add cream and boil until reduced to 1 cup. Pour over fish.

Serves 6

Baked Flounder with Vegetables

2 green peppers, sliced
1 cup zucchini, sliced
2 tomatoes, sliced
2 onions, sliced
1½ pounds flounder fillets
¼ teaspoon salt
¼ teaspoon pepper
½ cup water
1 tablespoon butter
¼ teaspoon paprika

1) Place one-half of the vegetables in a baking dish.

2) Season the flounder fillets with the salt and pepper, and place them on top of the vegetables.

3) Cover the fish with the remaining vegetables.

4) Pour in the water, dot with butter, and sprinkle with paprika.

5) Bake at 350 degrees for 20 minutes or until the fish flakes easily with a fork.

Serves 4

Baked Haddock with Cream

2 pounds haddock fillets
2 small red onions, thinly sliced
2 small tomatoes, sliced
3 cups cream
salt
pepper
thyme

1) Place the haddock fillets in a greased baking dish.

2) Cover the fish with the slices of onion.

3) Place another layer of fish on top of the onion.

4) Cover the second layer with the slices of tomato.

5) Sprinkle with salt, pepper, and thyme, and pour on the cream.

6) Bake at 375 degrees for 15 minutes, or until fish flakes easily with a fork.

Serves 6

Curried Halibut

1½ pounds halibut fillets, skinned
⅔ cup onion, sliced
⅔ cup celery, sliced
½ tablespoon cooking oil
1 teaspoon curry powder
½ teaspoon salt
pinch of pepper
½ cup skim milk
paprika

1) Place halibut fillets in an oiled baking dish.

2) Fry the onion and celery onion in oil for 4 to 5 minutes.

3) Stir in the seasoning and milk and place over fish.

4) Bake at 350 degrees for 25 minutes or until fish flakes easily when tested with a fork. Sprinkle with paprika.

Serves 4

Baked Halibut and Ratatouille

2 small zucchini, sliced
1 medium eggplant, cubed
1 red bell pepper, seeded and thinly sliced
1 yellow bell pepper, seeded and thinly sliced
1 tablespoon fresh oregano leaves
3 tablespoons fresh basil leaves
3 tablespoons olive oil
2 pounds frozen halibut fillets
salt
pepper

1) In a shallow baking dish combine zucchini, eggplant, red and yellow bell peppers, oregano, basil, and olive oil. Cover and bake in a 425 degree oven for approximately 40 minutes.

2) Mix the vegetables and move them to the sides of the baking dish.

3) Place the frozen halibut in the center of the dish.

4) Cover and bake for approximately 20 minutes or until fish flakes easily when tested with a fork. Season with salt and pepper if needed.

Serves 6

Spicy Mahi Mahi

2 pounds mahi mahi fillets
⅓ cup melted butter or margarine
4 tablespoons lemon juice
2 teaspoons dill weed
4 tablespoons chives
4 tablespoons parsley, chopped
½ teaspoon cayenne

1) Stir melted butter, lemon juice, dill weed, parsley, chives, and cayenne over medium flame for one minute. Let sit.

2) Place mahi mahi in a baking pan. Pour mixture over fish.

3) Bake uncovered in a 400 degree oven for 10 minutes or until fish flakes easily when tested with a fork.

4) Place fish on a warm platter and keep warm.

5) Broil the excess juices in a pan over high flame, stirring occasionally, until reduced to ½ cup. Pour over the fish.

Serves 6

Roasted Salmon with Peppercorns

3 pound whole salmon, gutted and scaled with head left on
½ teaspoon dried black peppercorns
½ teaspoon dried white peppercorns
½ teaspoon dried green peppercorns
¼ teaspoon salt
dash of cayenne pepper
1 tablespoon extra-virgin olive oil
2 tablespoons fresh lemon juice
2 tablespoons rosemary
2 small garlic cloves, unpeeled
fresh parsley

1) With a sharp knife, cut the salmon diagonally on the top side, making cuts one-half inch apart down the length of the fish, while cutting one-half inch deep.

2) Mix the peppercorns, salt, pepper, olive oil, and lemon juice together. Rub the mixture into the cuts and over the bottom side of the salmon.

3) Place the rosemary and garlic into the cavity of the salmon and marinate in the refrigerator for approximately 1 hour.

4) Place the salmon on a rack over a large roasting pan in a preheated oven at 425 degrees. Roast uncovered for 10 minutes per inch of thickness.

5) Remove the salmon from the oven and garnish with fresh parsley.

Serves 6

Salmon Casserole

1 (15½ oz.) can pink salmon
1 cup crackers, crushed
¼ cup butter
1 cup Swanson's clear chicken broth

1) Mix crackers with salmon, add chicken broth and melted butter.

2) Put in baking dish and bake uncovered at 350 degrees for 30 minutes.

Serves 2

Vera E. Henry
Medford, OR

Stuffed Sea Trout

2 3-pound sea trout
butter
salt
freshly ground black pepper
1½ cloves garlic, minced
2 medium onions, chopped
1½ cup cucumber, minced
¾ cup toasted almonds, chopped
6 cups dry bread crumbs
2 teaspoons thyme
sherry

For each fish:

1) Rub the inside of the trout with butter, salt, and pepper.

2) Saute the garlic and onion in butter until they are soft. Add them to the cucumber, almonds, and bread crumbs. Season with salt, pepper, and thyme.

Stuff the trout with mixture and sew it up. Place the stuffed fish on a well-oiled baking pan, season it with salt and pepper, adding small amount of sherry to the pan.

4) Bake the stuffed fish in a 425 degree oven and cook for approximately 30 minutes or until fish flakes easily when tested with a fork. Continue to add wine and butter when necessary, and baste with juices from the pan often.

Serves 6

Sole with Broccoli

1½ pounds sole fillets
20 ounces frozen broccoli spears
2 tablespoons flour
½ teaspoon salt
¼ teaspoon pepper
½ tablespoon melted butter or margarine
½ cup skim milk
¼ cup grated cheddar cheese
1 pound tomatoes, chopped

1) Cut sole fillets into six portions.

2) Cook broccoli for only one-half as long as is directed on the package. After draining, place broccoli in an oiled baking dish.

3) Place sole fillets over the broccoli.

4) Blend the seasonings and the flour into the melted butter. Slowly add in the milk, cook the mixture, stirring constantly until it is fairly thick and smooth. Add the cheese and stir into mixture until melted. Stir in the tomatoes.

5) Pour the sauce over the sole fillets.

6) Bake at 350 degrees for 20-25 minutes or until fish flakes easily when tested with a fork.

Serves 4

Baked Swordfish A La Sally

4 steaks
flour
oil
fresh dill
sliced onions
butter or margarine
salt
freshly ground black pepper
2 cups white wine
6 egg yolks
2 cups cream

1) Lightly dust the swordfish in flour and brush with oil.

2) Place two steaks in the bottom of a well-greased baking dish and spread them with a layer of fresh dill and a layer of sliced onions. Dot with butter and season with salt and pepper.

3) Place the other two steaks on top of the first two, also dotting these with butter and seasonings.

4) Pour 1 cup of the wine into the pan and bake at 425 degrees for 10 minutes per inch of fish or until fish flakes easily when tested with a fork. Baste the swordfish a number of times while baking.

5) When done, remove the steaks and place them on a hot platter. Add the remaining cup of wine to the pan, bringing it to a boil, and slowly stir in the cream mixed with the egg yolks. Stir until thick and smooth. Pour the mixture over the fish and serve.

Serves 4

Trustworthy Tuna Loaf

15 ounces canned tuna, drained and flaked
1 tablespoon lemon juice
½ teaspoon hot pepper sauce
½ teaspoon dill weed
2 cups fresh white bread crumbs
½ cup milk
3 eggs, separated

1) Preheat oven to 375 degrees.

2) Mix tuna, lemon juice, hot pepper sauce, dill weed, bread crumbs, milk, and egg yolks.

3) Beat egg whites until stiff, then fold into tuna mixture. Place mixture into an oiled loaf baking pan.

4) Bake for 30 to 35 minutes.

Serves 6

Tuna Casserole

2 cans (6½ oz.) water packed tuna
1 (11½ oz.) can cream of celery soup
2 celery stalks, chopped
1 can sliced black olives (2.2 oz.)
¼ cup chopped onion
¼ cup milk
1 teaspoon pepper
1 teaspoon seasonal salt
½ teaspoon garlic salt
1 (12 oz.) package egg noodles, cooked
1 cup bread crumbs (for topping)
1 cup mild cheddar cheese, grated

1) Mix all ingredients together in casserole dish and add the cooked egg noodles.

2) Top mixture with bread crumbs and cheese.

3) Bake at 375 degrees for 30 minutes or until cheese is melted. (Add green pepper, broccoli or carrots for variety).

Serves 4 to 5

Mrs. Cheryll Lippy
Bremerton, WA

Freshwater Whitefish Supreme

1½ pounds whitefish fillets, skinned
½ teaspoon salt
¼ teaspoon pepper
5 oz. instant mashed potato flakes
½ oz. garlic salad dressing mix
1 egg, beaten
⅛ cup butter or margarine
dash of paprika

1) Cut whitefish fillets into 4 portions.

2) Season the whitefish with salt and pepper.

3) Combine the potato flakes and the salad dressing mix.

4) Dip the fillets into the beaten egg and roll in the potato mixture.

5) Place the whitefish in a well-oiled baking pan. Pour the melted butter over the fillets and sprinkle with paprika.

6) Bake at 500 degrees for 10 minutes or until fish flakes easily when tested with a fork.

Serves 4

BOILED, POACHED, SIMMERED AND STEAMED

Poached Catfish in White Wine

6 catfish, dressed, with tails left on
6 green onions, sliced thinly
1½ teaspoon Worcestershire
1 garlic clove, crushed
¾ cup dry white wine
¾ cup water
1 teaspoon salt
sliced lemon

1) Place green onions, Worcestershire, garlic, wine, water, and salt in a pan and bring to a boil.

2) Add 3 catfish and bring to a boil once again. Reduce heat, cover, and simmer for approximately 10 minutes or until fish flakes easily when tested with a fork.

3) Place fish on a heated platter to keep warm. Repeat once again with the remaining catfish.

4) Pour pan liquid over fish, and garnish with lemon slices.

Serves 6

Cod Creole

1 pound cod fillets
⅓ cup chopped celery
1 medium onion, chopped
¾ cup chopped green pepper
½ tablespoon butter
6 ounces tomato sauce
½ teaspoon curry powder
¼ teaspoon salt
⅛ teaspoon pepper

1) Saute the celery, onion, and green pepper in butter. Stir in the rest of the ingredients with the exception of the cod.

2) Place the cod fillets in the mixture, cover and boil. Lower flame and simmer for 10 minutes per inch of fish thickness or until fish flakes easily when tested with a fork.

Serves 4

Smoked Cod

2 pounds smoked cod
6 cups water
1 teaspoon salt
2 hard-boiled eggs, chopped
¾ cup butter, melted

1) Skin the cod and cut into pieces.

2) Boil the water, add salt and cod. Simmer on low flame for approximately 10 minutes or until fish flakes easily when tested with a fork.

3) Mix the chopped eggs into melted butter, pour over fish and serve.

Serves 6

Cod with Mushrooms and Tomatoes

1¼ pounds cod fillets, cut into 1 to 2 inch strips
1 teaspoon unsalted sweet butter
1 pound fresh mushrooms, chopped
2 medium leeks, trimmed and sliced thinly
2 large shallots, chopped
2 scallions, sliced thinly
2 tomatoes, seeded and chopped
2 teaspoons dried thyme
2 tablespoons fresh parsley, chopped
1 teaspoon dried marjoram
4 tablespoons water
1½ cups light cream
dash of salt
dash of ground white pepper
watercress

1) Place butter, mushrooms, leeks, shallots, scallions, tomatoes, and herbs in water and cook slowly for 5 to 7 minutes or until liquid has evaporated.

2) Add cream to the mixture and simmer on low flame.

3) Lightly season the cod with salt and pepper, then place in the mixture. Sprinkle the sauce over the cod and cook, turning once for 5 to 10 minutes or until fish flakes easily when tested with a fork. Garnish with watercress and serve.

Serves 4

Cod Simmered with Tomato

2 pounds cod fillets
2 chopped tomatoes
1½ tablespoon onion, minced
¼ teaspoon basil
oil
salt
pepper
½ teaspoon dill weed
1 tablespoon butter
1½ tablespoon lemon juice
3 ounces water

1) Mix tomato, onion, and basil together and set aside.

2) Brush cod fillets lightly with oil and sprinkle with salt and pepper.

3) Stuff the centers of the fillets with the tomato mixture.

4) Saute onion in butter in frying pan. Place the cod fillets in the pan, add water and lemon juice, and simmer for approximately ten minutes until fish flakes easily when tested with a fork.

Serves 6

Halibut with Lemon Sauce

1½ pounds halibut fillets
3 tablespoons fresh lemon juice
1 tablespoon butter, melted
1½ tablespoons flour
1½ cups water
2 chicken bouillon cubes
3 egg yolks
dash of hot sauce

1) Cook flour in melted butter for one minute. Stir until well blended.

2) Slowly add in lemon juice, water, and bouillon cubes. Cook until mixture begins to thicken, stirring often. Remove and let stand.

3) Lightly beat egg yolks and hot sauce together. Mix egg and hot sauce into lemon mixture. Cook over low flame, stirring often, until the mixture begins to thicken.

4) Simmer halibut in enough water to cover the fish for approximately 10 minutes or until fish flakes easily when tested with a fork.

5) Place halibut on a platter, pour lemon sauce over the fish and serve.

Serves 6

Halibut Poached in Clam Broth

2 pounds halibut
1¼ cups clam juice
1 shallot, minced
¼ teaspoon dried basil
dash of salt
dash of pepper

1) Place halibut fillets in a well-oiled pan and warm slightly on both sides.

2) Combine the clam juice, shallot, basil, and salt and pepper and pour over the halibut.

3) Cover and poach for 5 to 10 minutes or until fish flakes easily when tested with a fork.

Serves 6

Steamed Red Snapper

2 3-pound red snapper, peeled and scaled with head left on
salt
⅓ cup fresh ginger, peeled and grated
15 scallions, sliced thinly
12 mushrooms (shitake if available)
¼ cup soy sauce
¼ cup peanut oil
parsley

For each fish:

1) Cut two large "X's" into each side of the fish, approximately ½ inch deep. Rub with salt inside and out. Press the ginger and ¼ of the scallions into the cuts.

2) Place fish in steamer with mushrooms on top. Steam for 10 minutes per inch of fish thickness or fish flakes easily when tested with a fork.

3) Heat the peanut oil.

4) Pour soy sauce over the cooked fish, and place the remaining scallions on top. Pour the hot peanut oil over the fish so that the scallions sizzle.

5) Garnish with parsley and serve.

Serves 6

Poached Red Snapper

2 pounds red snapper fillets
2 small onions, chopped
6 lemon slices
1½ tablespoons chopped parsley
1½ teaspoons chopped dill weed
1 teaspoon salt
½ teaspoon pepper
water

1) Boil all of the ingredients with the exception of the fish in one inch of water.

2) Place the red snapper in the pan, cover and simmer for approximately 5 to 8 minutes or until fish flakes easily when tested with a fork.

Serves 6

Red Snapper Wrapped in Swiss Chard

1¼ pounds red snapper fillets
dash of salt
dash of ground black pepper
1 tablespoon unsalted sweet butter
1 teaspoon grated lemon rind
10 ounces Swiss chard, white rib removed

1) Blanch the Swiss chard for one minute.

2) Lightly season the red snapper with salt and pepper, dot with butter, sprinkle with lemon rind, and wrap with the blanched leaves of the Swiss chard.

3) Place red snapper in steamer and cook for 10 minutes per inch of fish thickness or until fish flakes easily when tested with a fork.

Serves 4

Don Quixote-Style Rockfish Stew

3 tablespoons olive oil
2 medium sized onions, chopped
2 large celery stalk, chopped
2 garlic cloves, minced
1 large green pepper, chopped
1 pound canned chick peas
2 bay leaves
¼ teaspoon dried oregano
1 tablespoon dark brown sugar
1½ tablespoon lemon juice
⅔ cup dry red wine
4 cups water
2 large tomatoes, cubed
1 cup sliced fresh mushrooms
dash of salt
dash of pepper
1½ pounds rockfish chunks

1) Heat olive oil in large pot and add onions, celery, garlic, and green pepper. Saute until the vegetables begin to soften.

2) Add chick peas, bay leaves, oregano, brown sugar, lemon juice, red wine, and water. Simmer for approximately 10 minutes.

3) Add tomatoes, mushrooms, salt, pepper, and simmer for another 5 minutes.

4) Stir the rockfish into the stew, cover, and simmer for 12 to 15 minutes or until fish flakes easily when tested with a fork.

Serves 6

Whole Salmon Poached in Chicken Broth

1 4-pound cleaned and dressed salmon with head left on
4 quarts chicken broth
lemon slices

1) Place the salmon in a fish poacher.

2) Quickly boil the chicken broth.

3) Pour the hot chicken broth over the salmon and cover tightly for 10 minutes per inch of fish thickness or until fish flakes easily when tested with a fork.

4) Remove salmon, garnish with lemon wedges and serve. Use broth as a gravy if desired.

Serves 4

Sensational Poached Sole

1 pound sole fillets
1 tablespoon vegetable oil
2 tablespoons lemon juice
1 onion, sliced
¼ teaspoon paprika
½ teaspoon dried marjoram
dash of salt
water

1) Place oil, lemon juice, onion, paprika, marjoram, and salt in a large pan.

2) Lay sole on top of ingredients, add enough water to cover the fish, and simmer 10 minutes per inch of fish thickness or until fish flakes easily when tested with a fork.

Serves 4

Swordfish Simmered with Vegetables

2 pounds swordfish
2 chicken bouillon cubes
½ cup boiled water
15 ounces canned stewed tomatoes
2 large carrots, sliced
½ cabbage, sliced

1) Place bouillon cube in hot water.

2) Place tomatoes, carrots, and cabbage in bouillon and simmer for approximately 20 minutes or until cabbage is tender.

3) Place swordfish over vegetables and simmer for 10 minutes per inch of fish thickness or until fish flakes easily when tested with a fork.

Serves 4

BROILED

Sassy Bass

2 pounds bass fillets
¾ cup port
1½ teaspoons garlic powder
½ teaspoon cayenne pepper
1½ teaspoons rosemary
fresh parsley

1) Blend the port, garlic powder, cayenne, and rosemary together.

2) Spread the sauce over the bass and place in a marinating dish with any leftover sauce in the refrigerator for 45 minutes. Make sure to turn the fillets a few times while marinating.

3) Place the marinated bass in a preheated, lightly oiled broiler pan and broil for approximately 5 to 10 minutes or until fish flakes easily when tested with a fork. Baste occasionally during cooking. Garnish with fresh parsley.

Serves 6

Spicy Cod Amadine

1½ pounds cod fillets
¼ cup flour
1 teaspoon paprika
¾ teaspoon all purpose seasoning
¼ cup butter, melted
½ cup sliced almonds
⅛ teaspoon hot pepper sauce
2 tablespoons lemon juice
1 tablespoon chopped parsley

1) Mix the flour, paprika, and seasoning. Roll the cod in the mixture.

2) Place the fillets, skin side down, in a well-oiled baking pan. Dot with one-half of the melted butter.

3) Broil for approximately 10 minutes or until fish flakes easily when tested with a fork.

4) Saute the almonds in the remaining melted butter.

5) Blend in the hot pepper sauce, lemon juice, and parsley. Spoon over the broiled cod and serve.

Serves 4

Drum with Four-Spice

2 pounds drum fillets
4 scallions, sliced and crushed
8 slices fresh ginger, crushed
2 tablespoons rice wine
⅓ cup soy sauce
1 tablespoon sesame oil
1½ tablespoons sugar
⅛ teaspoon ground allspice
⅛ teaspoon anise seeds, crushed
⅛ teaspoon ground cloves
⅛ teaspoon ground cinnamon

1) Blend scallions, ginger, rice wine, soy sauce, sesame oil, sugar, and four spices together.

2) Lay drum in marinating dish and pour sauce our fish. Place in refrigerator and let marinate for 6 hours.

3) Place marinated drum on broiler and cook for 10 minutes or until fish flakes easily when tested with a fork.

Serves 6

Halibut Au Moutarde

6 halibut fillets
¾ teaspoon dijon mustard
½ cup mayonnaise
¼ teaspoon all-purpose seasoning
¼ teaspoon pepper

1) Mix mustard, mayonnaise, seasoning, and pepper together.

2) Place halibut fillets on a lightly oiled broiled rack for 8 to 10 minutes or until fish flakes easily when tested with a fork.

3) Spread the halibut fillets with the mustard mixture, and broil until mustard mixture begins to brown and bubble.

Serves 6

Halibut in Citrus Sauce

2 pounds halibut fillets
½ cup butter, melted
¾ teaspoon grated lemon rind
¾ teaspoon grated orange rind
5 tablespoons lemon juice
¼ teaspoon freshly ground black pepper

1) Blend lemon rind, orange rind, lemon juice, and black pepper into the melted butter.

2) Place the halibut in a warm broiler pan, brush with the citrus sauce and cook, basting frequently for 5 to 10 minutes or until the fish flakes easily when tested with a fork.

Serves 6

Grilled Smoked Mackerel

Use a good scale fish, leave scales on. Wash and pat dry. Sprinkle well with seasoning salt. Place on grill and cook until done—20 to 30 minutes, according to size of fish.

When done, place fish on serving dish and garnish with fresh parsley and lemon wedges. Serve with green salad and barbecue bread.

Allow 1 lb. of fish per serving. Tuna, salmon or mackerel are equally delicious.

Jennie C. Sloan
Bay Minette, AL

Mullet on Fire

2 pounds mullet fillets
⅓ cup sherry
¾ teaspoon dried tarragon
¼ teaspoon ground ginger
½ teaspoon garlic powder
fresh parsley

1) Blend the sherry, tarragon, ginger, and garlic powder together.

2) Spread the sauce over the mullet and place in a marinating dish with any leftover sauce in the refrigerator for 45 minutes. Make sure to turn the fillets a few times while marinating.

3) Place the marinated mullet in a preheated, lightly oiled broiler pan and broil for approximately 5 to 10 minutes or until fish flakes easily when tested with a fork. Baste occasionally during cooking. Garnish with fresh parsley.

Serves 6

Red Snapper A La California

6 red snapper steaks
½ cup fresh lime juice
½ cup salad oil
4 canned whole green chilis, seeded and sliced crosswise
¾ teaspoon oregano leaves
¼ teaspoon crushed red pepper
½ teaspoon sugar
1 teaspoon salt

1) Mix all of the ingredients together.

2) Place red snapper in a marinating dish, pour mixtur over fish and marinate for 2 to 4 hours. Turn fillets a number of times while marinating.

3) Broil marinated fillets in pre-heated broiler for 10 minutes or until fish flakes easily when tested with a fork. Baste often with remaining sauce.

Serves 6

Rockfish with Paprika

1½ pounds rockfish steaks
2 tablespoons butter, melted
1 tablespoon paprika
salt
pepper

1) Place the rockfish steaks lightly greased broiler pan. Brush the steaks with about half the melted butter and sprinkle with paprika, salt and pepper.

2) Broil for 10 minutes, turn over, brush with remaining butter, and sprinkle again with paprika, salt and pepper. Broil for another 10 minutes or until the fish flakes easily when tested with a fork.

Serves 4

Salmon Marinated in Lime

2 pounds salmon fillets
all-purpose seasoning
freshly ground black pepper
¼ cup lime juice
1 tablespoon paprika
2 tablespoons butter, melted

1) Place fillets in a marinating dish. Sprinkle with seasoning and pepper. Spoon lime juice over salmon and let marinate for 45 minutes, turning once.

2) Place salmon on a well-oiled broiler pan.

3) Mix melted butter with leftover marinating juice. Brush fish with this sauce and sprinkle with paprika.

4) Broil for 10 minutes or until fish flakes easily when tested with a fork.

Serves 6

Lightly Seasoned Trout

1½ pounds trout fillets
1 teaspoon lemon juice
¼ cup butter, melted
teaspoon of paprika
slices of lemon
sprigs of thyme

1) Mix lemon juice and melted butter together.

2) Pour mixture over trout and sprinkle with paprika.

3) Broil for approximately 10 minutes or until fish flakes easily when tested with a fork. Garnish with slices of lemon and fresh sprigs of thyme.

Serves 4

Broiled Swordfish with Black Olives

2 pounds swordfish fillets
1½ cup black olives, drained, pitted and chopped
½ cup unsalted sweet butter
½ teaspoon freshly ground black pepper
½ cup chopped Italian parsley

1) Mix the olives, butter, pepper, and parsley.

2) On a well-oiled grill, cook the swordfish for 10 minutes per inch of fish thickness or until the fish flakes easily when tested with a fork.

3) Spread the olive mixture over the cooked fish and place in a warm oven until the mixture begins to melt.

Serves 6

Broiled Whitefish in a Tangy Sauce

2 pounds whitefish fillets
1½ tablespoons lemon juice
pinch of freshly ground black pepper
4 tablespoons butter, melted
1 large onion, chopped finely
1½ tablespoon parsley leaves, chopped

1) Blend the lemon juice, pepper, and melted butter together.

2) Place whitefish fillets in a warm broiler pan, with th skin side down. Lightly brush the fish with the butter sauce.

3) Broil for 3 minutes, then sprinkle with onion and parsley and continue cooking for approximately 5 minutes or until fish flakes easily when tested with a fork.

4) Reheat any leftover butter sauce and pour over the broiled whitefish.

Serves 6

DEEP FRIED, PAN FRIED, AND SAUTEED

Striped Bass with Raspberries

1⅓ pounds striped bass fillets
4 shallots, chopped
2 tablespoons butter
1 cup raspberry wine vinegar
2 tablespoons heavy cream
2 tablespoons fresh thyme, chopped
fresh raspberries

1) Saute the shallots in butter for 3 minutes.

2) Add ¾ cup of the raspberry wine vinegar and reduce over a high flame until about 1 tablespoon of liquid remains. It should resemble a glaze.

3) Add the striped bass fillets and cook 3 to 5 minutes on each side over a medium flame.

4) Remove fillets. Add remaining ¼ cup of raspberry wine vinegar to the pan. Reduce for 12 to 15 minutes over a high flame.

5) Add the heavy cream and stir until thoroughly heated and pour over the fillets. Garnish with fresh thyme and raspberries and serve immediately.

Serves 4

Fried Catfish

4 medium catfish
4 tablespoons butter
4 tablespoons flour
¼ teaspoon salt
½ teaspoon dried thyme
4 tablespoons parsley, chopped
4 tablespoons fresh lemon juice

1) Dust the catfish in flour seasoned with salt and thyme and place in a hot frying pan coated with melted butter.

2) Cook over medium flame for 5 minutes on each side. Place in a 400 degree oven until catfish flakes easily when tested with a fork.

3) Place the parsley and lemon juice in the pan that was used to cook the catfish and heat until warm. Then pour pan juices over the fish and serve.

Serves 4

Deep Fried Halibut

Approx. 10 strips Halibut, 6 x 1½ inches
1½ cups flour
½ teaspoon garlic powder
⅛ teaspoon oregano
1 tablespoon lemon juice
1 teaspoon lemon & herb seasoning salt
½ teaspoon salt

1) Mix breading ingredients thoroughly with ½ cup water.

2) Wash and dry halibut, dip in mixture.

3) Fry in hot oil until done. If needed, add more salt to halibut slices.

Serves 2

Bertha M. Larson
Wrongell, AK

Garlic Rockfish

1 pound rockfish fillets
8 large garlic cloves, sliced thinly
2 tablespoons extra-virgin olive oil
½ cup flour
pinch of salt
dash of pepper
lime wedges

1) Saute the garlic in the olive oil. Remove before the garlic browns.

2) Dust the rockfish fillets in flour seasoned with salt and pepper. Place the fillets in the hot oil and sauce over medium flame for 5 minutes on each side or until fish flakes easily when tested with a fork.

3) Reheat the garlic in the pan. Season and serve with wedges of lime.

Serves 4

Salmon A La Susanne

8 salmon, cleaned and dressed
2 tablespoons butter
2 tablespoons olive oil
1 cup flour
dash of salt
dash of pepper
2 eggs, beaten
1½ cups breadcrumbs, crushed

1) Heat the butter and olive oil in a large frying pan.

2) Lightly dust the salmon with flour, sprinkle with salt and pepper, and dip into the egg and breadcrumbs.

3) Saute quickly in the hot butter and oil for 5 minutes on each side.

Serves 4

Fried Salmon Southern Style

4 salmon, skinned and dressed
2 teaspoons salt
½ teaspoon pepper
2 eggs, beaten
2 tablespoons milk
2 cups cornmeal
melted fat

1) Lightly dust salmon with salt and pepper.

2) Mix eggs and milk together. Dip salmon in mixture and coat with cornmeal.

3) Fry fish in melted fat on medium flame for 5 minutes on each side.

4) Pat dry with a paper towel and serve.

Serves 4

Spicy Red Snapper

2 pounds red snapper fillets
¾ cup yellow corn meal
⅓ cup flour
1 teaspoons paprika
½ teaspoon salt
½ teaspoon pepper
⅓ teaspoon celery salt
¼ teaspoon dry mustard
¼ teaspoon onion powder
¾ cup buttermilk
olive oil

1) Mix all of the dry ingredients together.

2) Dip the red snapper in the buttermilk, then coat with the dry mixture.

3) Fry the fillets in hot oil for 5 minutes on each side or until fish flakes easily when tested with a fork.

4) Pat dry with a paper towel and serve.

Serves 6

Deep Fried Sole

1 pound sole fillets
2 tablespoon cornmeal
2 teaspoons baking soda
2 teaspoons baking powder
2 cups flour
2 eggs
dash of beer
dash of salt
dash of pepper

1) Combine all of the ingredients with the exception of the fish and mix well until a thick batter forms.

2) Coat fish with mixture and deep fry for approximately 10 minutes.

Serves 4

Sole in White Wine

2 pounds sole fillets
1 cup flour
1 egg, beaten
1¼ cup fresh breadcrumbs
¼ cup butter
20 ounces fish stock
6 ounces white wine
20 ounces cream
2 teaspoons garlic, chopped
24 fresh basil leaves

1) Lightly dust the sole fillets with flour, then dip one side of each fillet in egg and breadcrumbs mixture.

2) Saute the fish in butter over medium heat for 5 minutes on each side.

3) In a different pan, reduce the fish stock and the white wine over medium flame until the mixture turns into a glaze. Add cream and reduce by half.

4) Add garlic and basil to the sauce and simmer over a low flame for 5 to 7 minutes.

5) Spoon sauce onto a warm serving plate, place the fish on top of the sauce, and serve.

Serves 6

Swordfish with Rosemary and Thyme

4½ pound swordfish steaks
1 cup flour
4 teaspoons dried rosemary
4 teaspoons dried thyme
2 tablespoons olive oil
⅓ cup butter
¾ cup white wine

1) Dust the steaks with flour and sprinkle with rosemary and thyme. Lightly press the rosemary and thyme into the flesh of the fish with your fingertips.

2) Lightly brush with oil and saute in butter for 5 minutes on each side or until fish flakes easily when tested with a fork.

3) Remove fish, add wine to pan juices, mix together and spoon over the fish.

Serves 4

Red Wine Swordfish

3 pounds swordfish steaks
¾ cup olive oil
4 large onions, sliced
½ cup all-purpose flour
1 cup red wine
1 tablespoon capers, drained
salt
pepper

1) Saute onions in ½ cup oil. Remove when slightly cooked, leaving oil in pan.

2) Coat steaks with flour, add remaining oil to skillet, and fry swordfish for 5 minutes on each side or until fish flakes easily when tested with a fork.

3) Combine swordfish and onions in skillet, add wine, capers, salt, and pepper. Cook for approximately 5 minutes. Chill and serve cold.

Serves 6

Classic Fried Trout

4 trout, cleaned and dressed
½ cup cornmeal
1½ tablespoons flour
dash of salt
dash of pepper
⅓ cup milk
1 teaspoon of olive oil
lemon wedges

1) Combine cornmeal, flour, salt and pepper.

2) Coat trout in milk, then dip in dry mixture. Let dry for 20 to 30 minutes.

3) Fry trout in heated oil for 5 minutes on each side. Pat dry on paper towels and serve with lemon wedges.

Serves 4

Tuna with Spaghetti

20 ounces tuna
1 16-ounce package spaghetti
¾ cup chopped onion
¾ cup chopped green pepper
⅓ cup olive oil
20 ounces tomato sauce
¾ cup water
¾ teaspoon garlic powder
1½ teaspoon oregano
2 teaspoons salt
½ teaspoon pepper

1) Saute the onion and green peppers in oil in a large frying pan.

2) Mix in the tuna fish, tomato sauce, water, garlic powder, oregano, salt and pepper. Cook for 10 minutes.

3) Pour tuna mixture over cooked spaghetti.

Serves 6

Yellowtail in White Wine

1 pound yellowtail fillets
1 tablespoon flour
1 egg
dash of salt
dash of pepper
3 tablespoons olive oil
2 ounces white wine
juice of 1 lemon
1 tablespoon parsley, chopped
½ tablespoon butter

1) Lightly dust the fillets with flour.

2) Combine egg, salt, and pepper and coat dusted fillets with mixture.

3) Cook fillets in heated olive oil over medium flame for 5 minutes on each side.

4) Combine white wine, lemon juice, parsley, and butter. Heat until mixture begins to thicken, then spoon over yellowtail and serve.

Serves 4

Yellowtail in Peanut Oil

1½ pounds yellowtail fillets
⅓ cup milk
2 egg yolks
⅛ teaspoon salt
⅛ teaspoon pepper
1 cup dry bread crumbs
1 cup peanut oil

1) Cut yellowtail fillets into ½ inch strips.

2) Mix milk, egg yolk, salt, and pepper together.

3) Place the strips of yellowtail into the mixture for 2 to 3 minutes.

4) Coat the soaked fillets with the bread crumbs, rolling each piece between your hands in order to get an evenly rounded strip.

5) Fry the coated fillets in the peanut oil for 3 to 5 minutes. Pat dry with paper towels.

Serves 6

SHELLFISH

BAKED

Baked Clams Columbus

4 cups minced clams
½ cup butter, melted
2 cups cracker crumbs
1 cup bread crumbs, toasted
⅛ teaspoon paprika
4 tablespoons onion, minced
4 tablespoons parsley, minced
½ cup cream

1) Mix the butter with the cracker and bread crumbs. Add the paprika. Set aside ⅓ cup of the mixture.

2) Mix the clams, onion, and parsley into the remaining mixture. Spoon into a well-oiled baking dish and top with the remaining crumb mixture. Spoon the cream over the top.

3) Bake in a preheated 375 degree oven for 25 minutes.

Serves 4

Spanish Clams

6 pounds clams in the shell
2 cups cooked tomatoes
2 cloves garlic, chopped finely
2 medium onions, chopped finely
1 slice smoked ham, shredded
2 pints fresh clam broth
⅛ teaspoon saffron
2 cups Spanish rice

1) Combine the tomatoes, garlic, onion, ham, and clam broth and simmer for 20 to 25 minutes. Add the saffron.

2) Clean the clams and place them in a casserole dish with the rice. Spoon the hot sauce over the clams.

3) Bake in a preheated 350 degree oven until the liquid is nearly all absorbed and the rice is cooked.

Serves 4

Baked Alaskan King Crab Legs

2 pounds Alaska king crab legs
butter, melted
lemon wedges

1) Slice legs into serving pieces, approximately 3 inches long. Cut the tops of the pieces lengthwise and lay on a sheet of aluminum foil.

2) Place the melted butter into the slits and seal the foil around the crab.

3) Bake in a preheated 400 degree oven for 10 minutes. Serve with melted butter and lemon wedges.

Serves 4

Spicy Crab

1 pound cooked or canned crab meat in small chunks
3 tablespoons butter
2 tablespoons chopped sweet green pepper
2 tablespoons minced onion
2 tablespoons all-purpose flour
½ cup milk
4 drops Tabasco sauce
1½ teaspoons Worcestershire sauce
1½ teaspoons dry mustard
¼ cup bread crumbs

1) Saute green pepper and onion in 2 tablespoons of butter.

2) Stir in the flour. Slowly mix in the milk until the sauce becomes smooth and thick. Stir in Tabasco, Worcestershire, and mustard.

3) Mix in the crab meat and divide into small, well-oiled custard cups.

4) Stir-fry bread crumbs in remaining tablespoon of butter and sprinkle over the crab mixture.

5) Bake in a preheated 375 degree oven for 20 minutes.

Serves 4

Baked Lobster with Garlic and Herbs

2 lobsters (2 pounds each)
5 tablespoons olive oil
2 cloves garlic, mixed
¼ teaspoon oregano
¼ teaspoon basil
¼ teaspoon parsley
8 tablespoons butter
1 cup bread crumbs

1) Slice the lobster and remove the intestinal tract. Lightly brush with the olive oil.

2) Saute the garlic and herbs for 5 minutes in 4 tablespoons of the butter and mix the bread crumbs. Spread the mixture over the lobster and dot with the remaining 4 tablespoons of butter.

3) Bake in a preheated 400 degree oven for 25 minutes.

Serves 4

Oysters Rockefeller

36 oysters, shelled, liquid and large halves of shell reserved
1 cup oyster liquid, strained
⅓ cup celery, minced
⅓ cup shallots, minced
¾ cup fresh spinach leaves, stemmed and minced
⅓ cup parsley leaves, minced
¾ teaspoon coffee liqueur
¾ teaspoon Tabasco sauce
10 tablespoons bread crumbs, lightly toasted
1 cup butter
lemon wedges

1) Saute celery, shallots, spinach, parsley, liqueur, Tabasco, and bread crumbs in ½ cup of butter over a medium flame for 5 minutes. Set aside.

2) Mix the oyster liquid and remaining ½ cup of buter together and cook over medium flame until hot. Stir and place into the oyster shells.

3) Place an oyster in each half shell. It should be floating in the buttery oyster liquid. Place the mixture that had been set aside over the oysters.

4) Bake in preheated 400 degree oven for 15 minutes. Serve with lemon wedges.

Serves 6

Baked Shrimp Supreme

3 pounds uncooked shrimp, peeled
½ cup peanut oil
5 tablespoons parsley, chopped
¾ cup flaked coconut
⅓ cup dry bread crumbs
½ teaspoon paprika
1½ tablespoons garlic, minced
⅛ teaspoon cayenne
¾ teaspoon salt
¾ cup sherry

1) Combine oil, parsley, coconut, bread crumbs, paprika, garlic, cayenne, and salt. Reserve ⅓ cup of mixture.

2) Toss shrimp in mixture until shrimp is well coated.

3) Place in a lightly greased casserole dish. Spoon sherry over shrimp and sprinkle with reserved mixture.

4) Bake uncovered at 375 degrees for approximately 45 minutes.

Serves 8-10

Baked and Stuffed Jumbo Shrimp

16 jumbo shrimp
8 tablespoons butter, melted
6 tablespoons chopped parsley
2 cups bread crumbs
½ cup flaked crab
½ cup chopped almond
½ cup sherry

1) Remove the shells of the shrimp up to the tails, slice the shrimps down the back in butterfly fashion and remove the large intestine.

2) Place shrimps in a baking dish with melted butter.

3) Combine parsley, bread crumbs, crab, almonds, and sherry. Stuff each shrimp with the mixture.

4) Place in a preheated 350 degree oven for 25 minutes.

Serves 4

Baked Butterfly Shrimp

12 large shrimp, peeled
6 tablespoons lemon juice
½ cup butter
1½ cup bread crumbs
5 cloves garlic, minced
3 teaspoons paprika
¾ cup chopped parsley

1) Remove the shells of the shrimp up to the tails, slice the shrimps down the back in butterfly fashion and remove the large intestine.

2) Sprinkle the shrimp with the lemon juice. Combine the butter, bread crumbs, garlic, paprika, and parsley. Spoon the mixture on each shrimp.

3) Bake at 400 degrees for 15 to 20 minutes.

Serves 6

BOILED, SIMMERED AND STEAMED

Clam Curry in a Hurry

2 cups cooked clams
⅓ cup flour
1½ cups milk
⅛ cup butter
1½ teaspoons curry powder
½ teaspoon dill weed
½ teaspoon salt
¾ cup pineapple, chopped

1) Blend flour, ½ cup milk, butter, curry, dill, and salt.

2) Slowly stir in the remaining milk.

3) Cook over low flame until mixture begins to boil and thicken. Stir often.

4) Add the clams and pineapple. Cook until heated.

Serves 4

Oriental Mussels

6 pounds mussels in shells, cleaned and bearded
3 tablespoons sesame oil
5 cloves garlic, chopped
4 tablespoons fresh ginger, minced
½ cup fresh cilantro, chopped
4 onions, sliced thinly
2 cups white wine
2 cups chicken broth
2 tablespoons soy sauce

1) Saute the garlic, ginger, cilantro, and onions in the oil.

2) Place the wine, broth, soy sauce, and mussels in a pot. Add the sauteed garlic and ginger.

Serves 6

Mussels Marinara Classique

6 pounds mussels, cleaned and bearded, in the shell
6 cups white wine

1) Heat white wine to boiling. Add mussels and lower flame.

2) Simmer until the mussels open, approximately 5 minutes.

3) Place mussels in a serving bowl. Strain the broth and pour over the mussels.

Serves 6

Mussels with Fettucini

2 dozen mussels, scrubbed and debearded, in the shell
1½ tablespoons butter, melted
⅓ cup mushrooms, sliced
⅓ cup baby carrots, sliced
⅓ cup snow pea pods
⅓ cup asparagus, sliced
½ cup light cream
¼ cup water
¼ cup dry white wine
dash of salt
¼ cup fresh parsley, chopped
½ pound fresh fettucini
⅛ teaspoon black pepper
½ cup Italian Parmesan cheese, grated

1) Saute the vegetables in the melted butter. Melt the butter and cook all the vegetables for 3 to 4 minutes.

2) Pour in the cream and cook until the mixture begins to thicken, approximately 5-7 minutes.

3) Place the mussels in a pot, add the water, wine, salt, and one-half of the parsley. Bring to a boil over medium flame. Remove the mussels and let stand.

4) Steam the mussels over a high flame until they open, approximately 5 minutes. Remove the mussels from the shells and add to the vegetable cream sauce.

5) Pour sauce over cooked fettucini. Add pepper and left over parsley. Sprinkle with the grated cheese.

Serves 2

Steamed Mussels Riviera

2 dozen mussels, scrubbed, debearded, in the shell
1 tablespoon butter
¼ cup finely chopped scallions
1 yellow bell pepper, chopped
⅛ cup minced shallots
1 teaspoon fresh basil
1 teaspoon fresh thyme
1 teaspoon orange rind, grated
¼ cup water
¾ cup dry white wine
¼ cup parsley, minced

1) Saute the onions in the butter. Add the rest of the ingredients with the exception of the mussels and bring to a boil over a medium flame.

2) Place the mussels in the pot, cover, and cook over medium flame until the mussels open, approximately 5 minutes.

3) Throw out any mussels that have not opened.

4) Place mussels in a serving bowl. Pour the steaming hot broth and the vegetables over the mussels. Sprinkle with parsley.

Serves 2

Hot and Spicy Oysters

1 pound fresh oysters, shucked, cleaned, and drained
¼ teaspoon Worcestershire sauce
¼ teaspoon cayenne pepper
¼ cup butter or margarine
juice of 1 lemon

1) Combine all of the ingredients with the exception of the oysters in a pot. Bring to a boil over medium flame.

2) Add the oysters. Simmer on a low flame, and poach for 4 to 5 minutes or until the edges of the oysters begin to curl.

3) Pour sauce over oysters and serve.

Serves 4

Shrimp Thailand

1 pound cooked shrimp
½ cup white vinegar
½ cup peanut oil
1½ teaspoons hot mustard
1 tablespoon chili sauce
1 small clove garlic
1 tablespoon chive, chopped
¼ teaspoon paprika

1) Combine all of the ingredients with the exception of the paprika. Mix well.

2) Toss in cooled shrimp. Cover and refrigerate for 4 to 5 hours, tossing occasionally.

3) Drain and sprinkle with paprika.

Serves 4

Shrimp Curry

3½ cups shrimp, boiled and deveined
½ cup butter or margarine
6 tablespoons flour
2 cups applesauce
1 package Lipton's Onion Soup Mix
2 cups water
½ teaspoon ginger
2 to 3 teaspoons curry powder
½ teaspoon lemon juice (to taste)

1) Melt butter in large pan and blend in flour. Stir in the applesauce, soup mix, water, curry powder, ginger and lemon juice.

2) Cook until it thickens to the correct consistency. Add shrimp and heat thoroughly. Serve over mounds of rice.

3) Sprinkle or pass condiments—shredded coconut, ground nuts and chutney.

Serves 8

Mrs. Harry H. Hall
Edinburg, TX

Shrimp on Fire

1 pound shrimp
1 small onion, sliced
1 teaspoon fresh thyme
1 teaspoon dry mustard
1 teaspoon hot sauce
1 cup chicken bouillon
¼ cup vinegar

1) Combine all of the ingredients in a pot. Bring to a boil and simmer over low flame until cooked—shrimp will be pink.

2) Remove, cool, and chill. Drain thoroughly and serve.

Serves 4

Hawaiian Shrimp

3 cups fresh pineapple, in chunks
4 tablespoons pickly syrup
dash of salt
¾ cup pickle, chopped
1½ tablespoons cornstarch, dissolved in water
1½ pounds shrimp, cooked

1) Place pineapple and juices, pickles, pickle syrup, dissolved corn starch, and salt in a pot. Bring mixture to a boil, until it thickens and begins to turn clear.

2) Add the cooked shrimp and heat until warm.

Serves 6

Seafood Sauce Picante

2 pounds shrimp
2 cans crab meat
¼ pound smoked sausage, sliced
salt and pepper
cayenne pepper
1 can tomatoes
2 onions, chopped
2 bell peppers, chopped
3 to 4 cups water
Creole Seasonings

1) Brown sausage. Add tomatoes, onions and bell peppers. Cook until thick.

2) Add 3 cups of water—more if needed—salt and pepper. Cook 15 minutes.

3) Add shrimp and crab meat, cook another 15 minutes Serve over cooked rice.

Serves 4

Mrs. Peter Ducote
Alexandria, LA

Jambalaya (with Shrimp)

2 pounds shrimp, in the shell
4 slices bacon, chopped
4 garlic cloves, chopped
1 cup onion, chopped
2 medium green peppers, chopped
½ teaspoon fresh basil
½ teaspoon chili powder
1 teaspoon Worcestershire sauce
¼ teaspoon pepper
2 pounds whole tomatoes, canned
2 cups rice

1) Simmer shrimp for 3 to 4 minutes, then peel, devein, and refrigerate.

2) Strain the broth, setting aside 4 cups.

3) Fry the bacon and add garlic, onion, and green pepper. Saute for 3 minutes. Add strained broth, basil, chili powder, Worcestershire, pepper, tomatoes, and rice. Bring to a boil, and simmer over a low flame.

4) Cover and cook. Add shrimp and ham for the final 3 minutes of cooking to heat. Cook until the rice is ready or nearly all of the liquid is absorbed Mix well and serve.

Serves 8

Shrimp Etouffe

3 lbs. shrimp, peeled and deveined
6 tablespoons butter
3 tablespoons flour
1 cup chopped onion
6 green onions, chopped
½ cup bell peppers, chopped
½ cup celery, chopped
2 cups water
¼ cup parsley, chopped
1 clove garlic, minced
dash red pepper
cooked rice

1) In a large iron skillet, melt butter and stir in flour. Cook, stirring constantly until this is a rich brown.

2) Saute onions, bell peppers and celery in another pan. Add vegetables (when softened), water, shrimp, parsley and seasoning to flour mixture and simmer for 20 minutes. Serve over hot cooked rice.

Serves 4-6

Eimilia Linder
W. Monroe, LA

BROILED

Clams with Bacon

3 dozens clams, shucked and drained
12 slices bacon, cut in thirds
lemon wedges

1) Wrap slices of bacon around the clams.

2) Broil for 3 to 5 minutes on each side or until bacon is crisp. Serve with lemon wedges.

Serves 6

Clams in Spicy Tomato Sauce

4 dozen clams, in the shell
6 tablespoons olive oil
2 onions, minced
2 garlic cloves, chopped
2 cups tomato paste
½ teaspoonn crushed red pepper
1 teaspoon fresh oregano
1 cup toasted bread crumbs
2 tablespoons butter

1) Steam clams until they open. Remove clams from shells. Reserve shells and 3 cups of strained broth.

2) Saute onion and garlic in olive oil.

3) Stir in tomato paste. Add clam broth, red pepper, oregano, and salt and bring to a boil. Lower flame and simmer for 15 to 20 minutes, stirring often.

4) Chop up the steamed clams and stir into sauce. Place in reserved shells, sprinkle with bread crumbs, dot with butter, and broil for 5 minutes or until brown.

Serves 4

Broiled Lobster

6 1½-pound lobsters, steamed
1½ cups butter, melted
lemon wedges

1) Split and clean the steamed lobsters.

2) Place on broiler pan, brush with melted butter, and cook until butter begins to brown. Continue to brush with butter while broiling. Serve with lemon wedges.

Serves 6

Oysters on the Half Shell

4 dozen oysters, in the shell
6 tablespoons olive oil
2 onions, minced
2 garlic cloves, chopped
2 cups tomato paste
½ teaspoon crushed red pepper
1 teaspoon fresh oregano
1 cup toasted bread crumbs
2 tablespoons butter

1) Steam oysters until they open. Remove oysters from shells. Reserve shells and 3 cups of strained broth.

2) Saute onion and garlic in olive oil.

3) Stir in tomato paste. Add oyster broth, red pepper, oregano, and salt and bring to a boil. Lower flame and simmer for 15 to 20 minutes, stirring often.

4) Chop up the steamed oysters and stir into sauce. Place in reserved shells, sprinkle with bread crumbs, dot with butter, and broil for 5 minutes or until brown.

Serves 4

Oysters in a Blanket

3 dozen oysters, shucked and drained
12 slices bacon, cut in thirds
lemon wedges

1) Wrap slices of bacon around the oysters.

2) Broil for 3 to 5 minutes on each side or until bacon is crisp. Serve with lemon wedges.

Serves 6

Oriental Shrimp

2 pounds shrimp, in the shell
1 cup soy sauce
1 cup sherry
2 tablespoons lemon juice
2 cloves garlic, crushed
⅓ cup peanut oil

1) Peel and devein shrimp.

2) Combine the remaining ingredients, spoon over shimp and refrigerate for 6 hours.

3) Place shrimp in broiler and cook for 3 minutes on each side.

Serves 6

DEEP FRIED, PAN FRIED, AND SAUTEED

Fettucini with Clams

2 tablespoons virgin olive oil
¾ cup garlic, minced
2 cups heavy cream
2 pounds raw clams, shucked and chopped
dash of salt
½ teaspoon ground pepper
1½ pounds fettucini, cooked and drained

1) Saute the garlic in the oil. Add the cream and cook over medium flame until mixture begins to thicken, approximately 8 to 10 minutes.

2) Add the clams, salt, and pepper and cook until thoroughly heated.

3) When the sauce is steaming hot, toss with the cooked fettucini.

Serves 6

Crab Cakes

1½ pounds crab meat
2 slices white bread with crusts removed, chopped
1 egg, beaten
½ tablespoon Worcestershire sauce
1 tablespoon mustard
dash of Tabasco sauce
½ cup mayonnaise
juice from 1 lemon
oil for frying

1) Gently mix all of the ingredients and shape into 8 large crab cakes.

2) Fry cakes in oil for 5 minutes on each side or until brown.

Serves 4

Crab and Linguini Feast

3 pounds crab meat
3 pounds fettucini, cooked and drained
4 tablespoons butter
12 scallions, chopped
6 large ripe tomatoes, peeled, seeded and chopped
dash of salt
½ teaspoon ground pepper
3 teaspoons fresh thyme, chopped
1½ cups light cream
2 egg yolks
½ cup Italian parsley, chopped

1) Saute the scallions in the butter. Add the tomatoes and herbs. Cook for 2 minutes.

2) Toss in the crab meat and cook until crab is thoroughly heated.

3) Mix in the cream with the egg yolk. Cook until the mixture is steaming hot.

4) Sprinkle with parsley. Pour the sauce on top of the cooked fettucini.

Serves 12

Louisiana Lobster

1 pound lobster meat, cooked
2 cloves garlic, chopped
2 green peppers, seeded and cut into strips
4 onions, chopped
6 tablespoons butter
2 cups tomato sauce
dash of salt
dash of pepper
dash of Cayenne pepper
½ cup heavy cream

1) Saute the garlic, green pepper, and onions in butter for 5 minutes. Mix in the tomato sauce and cook until reduced by one-quarter.

2) Stir in seasonings and cream. Add the lobster meat and cook until thoroughly heated.

Serves 4

Quick and Easy Lobster

1½ pounds boiled lobster, chopped
6 cups milk
¾ cup light cream
¼ teaspoon pepper
4 tablespoon butter

1) Place the lobster shells in the milk and scald the liquid.

2) Saute lobster in butter. Add the scalded milk and bring to a boil.

3) Remove from stove, pour cream over the lobster, and serve.

Serves 6

Skewered Oysters

4 dozen raw oysters
16 strips of bacon, sliced in thirds lengthwise and fried
2 eggs
1½ cups milk
½ cup flour
oil for frying

1) Place one-half dozen oysters and one-half dozen pieces of bacon on each skewer.

2) Combine the eggs and milk. Place the flour in a separate bowl.

3) Dip each skewer in the egg and milk batter, then dip in the flour.

4) Deep fry the coated oysters and bacon for approximately 5 minutes on each side or until brown.

Serves 4

Scallops in White Wine

1½ pounds scallops, rinsed
2 tablespoons flour
3 tablespoons olive oil
4 ounces butter
6 tablespoons onion, chopped
⅛ teaspoon cayenne pepper
⅛ teaspoon nutmeg
dash of salt
4 ounces white wine
10 ounces whipping cream
¾ cup sour cream
2 teaspoons parsley, chopped
2 tablespoons chives
juice from 1 lemon

1) Dust the scallops with flour. Place in pan with 2 ounces of butter and saute over medium flame for approximately 3 minutes on each side or until they begin to brown.

2) Add the chopped onion, cayenne, and nutmeg. Continue to saute for another 2 minutes.

3) Add the wine and continue cooking until wine is substantially reduced. Add the cream and cook for 3 more minutes. Remove from flame.

4) Stir in the sour cream, parsley, chives, remaining butter, and lemon juice.

Serves 4

Sauteed Scallops with Orange

1¼ pounds large scallops, rinsed and cut in half
2 cups bread crumbs
1 teaspoon fresh thyme
1 teaspoon fresh basil
1 teaspoon fresh marjoram
1 teaspoon fresh chives
2 tablespoons orange rind, chopped
dash of salt
½ teaspoon ground pepper
2 tablespoons butter
2 tablespoons virgin olive oil
4 tablespoons fresh parsley
1 dozen orange wedges, peeled

1) Combine the herbs, crumbs, salt, and pepper. Toss the scallops in the mixture.

2) Saute lightly coated scallops in the butter over medium flame for 7 to 8 minutes.

3) Garnish with parsley and arrange orange wedges around scallops.

Serves 4

Pan Fried Scallops

2 pounds scallops, rinsed
flour
6 tablespoons butter
dash of salt
¼ teaspoon pepper
⅓ cup parsley, chopped

1) Lightly dust the scallops with flour.

2) Saute the dusted scallops in the butter approximately 4 minutes on each side or until brown.

3) Sprinkle salt, pepper, and parsley and serve.

Serves 6

Sensational Sauteed Scallops

2 pounds scallops, rinsed
¾ cup bread crumbs
¼ teaspoon paprika
¼ teaspoon salt
¼ teaspoon pepper
½ cup butter
2 cups cooked rice
⅓ cup white wine

1) Mix the bread crumbs, paprika, salt, and pepper together. Dip the scallops in the mixture.

2) Saute the scallops in the butter for approximately 5 minutes or until brown. Remove and arrange on a bed of rice.

3) Add the white wine to the butter in the pan. Simmer and stir for 1 minute. Spoon over scallops.

Serves 6

Shrimp Scampi Classico

2 pounds shrimp, shelled
4 cloves garlic, crushed
3 tablespoons butter
2 eggs, beaten
½ cup white wine

1) Saute the garlic in the butter.

2) Dip the shrimp in the eggs and place in the butter and garlic. Saute over high flame for 4 to 5 minutes. Add white wine to pan and serve.

Serves 6

NOTES

NOTES

NOTES

NOTES

NOTES

NOTES